# AMALGAMATION

# AMALGAMATION

ROBERT WRIGHT & SADERIA CARTER

SJW

Omaha, Nebraska

AMALGAMATION

For publishing inquiries, contact:

Saderia Jeanpierre Wright LLC
c/o Concierge Marketing
4822 S. 133rd St.
Omaha, NE 68137
(402) 884-5995

B&W Paperback ISBN: 978-1-945505-24-9
Color Paperback ISBN: 978-1-945505-25-6
Kindle ISBN: 978-1-945505-26-3
EPUB ISBN: 978-1-945505-27-0

Publishing and production services by Concierge Marketing Inc.

Library of Congress Control Number: 2018902868
Cataloging-in-Publication data on file with the publisher.

Printed in the USA

10 9 8 7 6 5 4 3 2 1

# CONTENTS

# INTRODUCTION

Many words ascended to captivate this stunning collection. Among them were invigorating and nostalgic to explain the combination. Of all, love is the edge and outer core. Static and heart-palpitations, yearning. I have had many highs and lows, not to mention feelings of despair and hopelessness. Instead of life taking me for a journey against my will, holding my emotions to steer, with different sight, I decided to ride and enjoy the journey as it is. With or without the things, I think, are important to me. However, making sure that I am healthy, whole, while adoring myself. Playing the hand that's dealt, and not wishing on stars for something else. Elbow to my knee, I think and imagine me, worry free and without a doubt know that other natives of poetry can relate to my words of love, hurt, despair, hope, and happiness, as well as digging deep into all the other topics this compilation exhibits. I love that it comes full circle. Life is many things and so is poetry—colorful, lively—life. Out of the darkness and into the light, we write *Amalgamation*.

*Saderia Carter*

The need for a loving blend of life into the friendships you see before you feeds the hunger from within our very souls. I love my father and he has proven time and time again he still loves me no matter what I do. Sometimes I hated myself for not loving myself. My father allowed me to learn a hard lesson in life. You must first love him and learn to love yourself. Only then can you learn to love others. The taste of life is seeping back into my bosom. I'm preparing to embark on yet another journey in my life that will allow me to show how much I care for those whom I have yet to meet. Enjoy the blends of poetry of life, trials, tribulations, and answers to your deepest questions. I believe that an amalgamation of all nationalities will come together someday and give thanks for "Him" who gave all He had to free our souls, hearts, and minds from those who would keep us in turmoil and lost to His cause.

Never have so few given so much to so many. Enjoy our recipes for love, politics, epical, and uplifting poetry.

*Robert Wright*

# SCURRY

"Scurrying through life

       Makes you appreciate

              The very moment

                     You sit down."

# MY LOVE IS DA BOMB

My love for you is da bomb, girl.
You should try to see me in your world.
All the things you want and see,
I will deliver to you, for love, from me.
I was not this way when life took my hand,
but a mere little boy, now a man.
I could tell you why I love you so much.
I could tell you why I need your touch.
Love is simple; love is kind.
Love is "you," love is mine.
See I loved you before I met you, girl.
I loved your presence in this world.
I have so much love in my soul to give,
if you could feel my light of love to live.
My love for you is da bomb, girl.
You should try to see me in your world.

RW

# I REFUSE

I refuse to be another woman
Shackled by this word called love
Chained at the heart
And feet so bound it can only move
At the jerk of beckoning calls from a lover
Who has the combination
To every wind of moment
I refuse to be another woman
Chained by emotional off-sets
And mentally uncontrollable sickness
Invaded from every touch and passionate kiss
Virus of love felt even in the tip of my toes and tip of my nails
I refuse to be another woman
Captured from running from this word
Captured from future tears and upset tones
And a disrupted life—giving love a try
To love and then hate
To love and then dissipate
Fall into and fall out of
And into
And out of
Love
Highly favorable
And highly unfavored
To drive a sweet person mental
Just to keep the high of love
Fresh in mind
Fresh in heart, never changing
No rearranging
But to always love what the word
Really means, bring life to various situations
It's hard to find true love
The kind of love they call silver
The kind of love they call gold
For years to come
Till the face and hands are no longer young
And the knees are no longer strong
But gamble my heart
To be saved from heart failures
As long as I can hold my heart
I refuse to love

# LOVE ON STEROIDS

If kisses were water, I'd give you the sea.

If hugs were leaves, I'd give you a tree.

If LIFE was a planet, I'd give you the galaxies, and

If friendship was life, I'd give you mine gladly.

RW

# HEART IMPAIRMENT

I keep on thinking
That I could let you go
And I keep on screaming
Yet eager at the same time
Wishing that I could just depart
But the simple truth is
You're just like a breath of fresh air
When I inhale
I can't see the forest or the trees
All I see is you
Wishing I could hold you, everyday
Like there is nothing else
You're tattooed
Your name written in my soul
And I've lost control
Never had it like this
Wish I could just split
For fear that you would eventually
Impair me for life
Cripple me the more
To where no one else could get close
Step back
Let me just touch you—sometimes
Let me just hold you—sometimes
Let me just kiss you—sometimes

For I can't let my soul linger
Like this
I'm afraid I've got to step off
Cat and mouse is the game I'll
Play
So my heart can stay
Intact
I build a wall so I won't fall
In those words that are so lightly
Spoken
Words taken for granted
So many times people just fake it
I'm wondering
If I tore down my walls
Could life be as sweet as sugar
Or as bitter as lemons
Taking no chances
I'm afraid I've just got to step off
Cat and mouse is the game I'll
Play
So my heart can stay
Intact
I build a wall so I won't fall
My dream will not be my reality
Trying to escape a heart impairment

# HOME AGAIN

I take my kisses broken often stirred.
It's better that way.
She stared into my face with her
soft hazel brown eyes.
They were calm.
One question stood behind her face.
I left it unanswered because I was
caught up in her spell.
She had me in her web.
I was helpless like the fly,
and who does God favor
in the web?
Bodies lie intertwined on a bed of lust.
Vows exchanged silently in a glance.
A smile signs the contract,
an embrace closes the deal.
Her warm body pressed firmly against me.
She says she will soon be mine.
But I can't front; I want her even
more than perhaps she wants me.
It's been a while since we've
danced. Lost in her lips,
I am found. They hold and express
to me how they missed me there.
I smile in their presence because I'm home.

RW

# I CAN'T FIND MY LOVE

Where is my love?
Has he gone away
It seems that finding a good black man
Is easily hard to find
One with a hint of thug and with a lot of love
To give
His woman and his family
Where have they gone
Are they in hiding
Under too much thug and in bed with too many hugs
From other ethnicities
Don't get me wrong—I embrace race and I embrace diversity
But seeing my love in another tribe's arms
Is killing me
I lie in bed and wait to be blessed
However, I wait forever
Because he's lying on light skinned breast
Maybe I must modify and alter what I like
And lie
To myself and settle for what I do not desire
And lay with a man whom I do not aspire
The good ones are in hostage
Behind bars, dealing with the D.O.C.
Their mentality and way of life mimic imperfection
So now we wait until the sentence
Is up
Black women
We got to be strong
Possibly widen our zone
Our men have left us
for imprisonment
And for other cultures
Do they not love our strength
Do they not love our heritage
Do they not love the blackness
That we so proudly carry

# CAN I SPEND THE NIGHT?

Can I spend the night?
I promise to make it all right.
Girl, let me touch inside your soul.
Can I turn you on?
Maybe I was wrong to let you go.
I wasn't thinking right; you should know.
All the times I said goodbye,
was no reason to make you cry.
I'm trying to give you what you need.
Not wanting to let go; please…
stay with me?
Can I spend the night?
I promise to make it all right.

RW

# RELISH

You know how it seems that life nominates you
For tribulations and
Puts you in situations where you wonder
If life is really on your side
Some things just don't work
And some things just don't happen
And you mount up to be prone to life
And the fact that everything won't work out
The way you intend
Every man won't spoil you with sweet words
Like honey on soft bread
Every man won't telekinesis your thoughts
And listen while you talk
Every man won't understand
Where you're coming from
And why you think the way you do
And look at you
When you walk in a room
And stare until it's simply uncomfortable
To look
Every man won't look at you with adolescent eyes
With amazement
Feeling stomach crunches when you smile
Or with hungry intentions of expression
Priceless and unreal
But…
If something like this
Drops in your way
Amuse the simple idea that this doesn't come easy
And this doesn't come by works
But this chance
To enjoy life's sweet chances
Rare chances
I must relish

# WHERE IS LOVE?

I have surrendered my love, and kept it safe.
Locked in the deepest tower of my being.
It's waiting for your touch to set it free.
Don't you believe me?
Free the love that has been waiting a lifetime for you. It has been a prisoner
of my insecurities, my hate, my passion, and my guilt for so long that it's not strong enough.
I'm not strong enough to do it alone.
Love has been lost in my world, abandoned like a stray mutt.
Battered, broken, covered in shame.
A life without love will never be the same.
Like a dragon guarding its young, I have fought to keep love
safe amongst thieves. It was taken from me 3 times, and I, myself, left for dead.
"Where is Love?"
Since then I have lost my way, lost everything, so I pray.
I shall find it again, and I will not hold it so tight, because now I know love is in plain
sight.
I realize now what I didn't before.
Love is mine, love is in me. It has always been in me… I locked myself up, slowed
space, and time.
Not realizing love has always been mine… For whom shall I give it? The Lord only
knows…
So I ask for forgiveness and for Him to show me light.
So I can walk out of darkness and love with all my might.
Like a child forlorn,
I was lost but now I'm found…
Thank you, Lord, for keeping my feet… on the ground.

RW

# STANDING IN THE WIND

What can make me feel the way I do?
How do I control the very essence of my heart's desire?
Maybe if I stood in the wind
It could just blow away
My mind remembers and my heart faints
Like an addition that can't wait
To remember the very hands
That took me to another place
My eyes look to and from daily
Looking for a glimpse of that life
My heart still faints
My hands still shake
How do I control this heart's desire?
Maybe if I stood in the wind
It could blow away
My stomach turns with illness of separation
My dreams are invaded with your face
Persuaded
That the old life was not ours to falter
Still love is stubborn
And to kill myself would be an only solution
Or
I could just stand in the wind and it could just
B l o w  A w a y...

# HOW MUCH DO I LOVE HER?

I'd set the world on fire
and pour rain on a desert.
Pull down the moon over the sun
so the heat wouldn't get her.
Give her all of the hearts that cupid
had in store, and put a ring on her
finger and tell her that I have more.
Kiss her every morning just because
she is the most beautiful woman
there ever was…
Keep the love flowing throughout all
of our lives…
always knowing she is my true bride.
And, last but not least, I would give her
the pitter patter of tiny little feet—
down the hall, to the left, by the room filled with toys.
There she would be with her arms full of joy…

RW

# UNDER MY SKIN

I see you getting deep under my skin

Fulfilling pleasures deep within

I see you driving into my soul

He's under my skin

Is this actuality

Wanting to come in

Undeniably blatant and cannot be hid

Honeybees come sting me

An everlasting bond

Organs and testosterone

Waving in and out of control

# L.O.V.E.

**L** — Living my life with the woman I love.

**O** — Obedient to the love we share.

**V** — Voluntarily giving my love to you,

**E** — Every day of my life.

# IF I WAS YOUR WOMAN

If I was your woman, and you were my man
Every night would be flickering moonlight
With love making in the shadows
If I was your woman, and you were my man
Morning showers wouldn't be ordinary
Evening dinner would be on edge
Seeing your face and pulling your hair
Kissing your lips wouldn't even compare
Hearing your voice in my ears
And words that pump blood into my hormones
But, only if I was your woman, and you were my man

# SHOT BY LOVE

Wind out of my chest,
because out of all of them,
you were my best.

Stricken with a blow,
that would topple any foe.
No chance for the flower to grow.

Thought the love could withstand
any pain, yet I fail…one in the same.
Looking forward, confident, I knew,
but love still hurts when the wind blows through.

# SQUANDERED

I hoped
I was the diamond in your rough
I hoped
I was the sunset in your morning
I hoped
You were fighting yourself
To keep from loving me
I hoped
That one day
You would come to me and
say I love you
I hoped
you would say
I love everything about you
I love your smile, your touch
I hoped
I was favored
And that somehow I was different
From anyone else
You know, every girl's fantasy
You were the game that I played into
I was your game piece
I was your imitation of counterfeit keen love
Such a fool
Such a waste
Squanderous player mate—losing another piece of my value

# TO KILL A BUTTERFLY

Once so very precious with all
  of her beauty…
    Elongated wings;
      such a real cutie.
      Didn't see you fly past my way,
        foot to the pedal, grinding
          away
            I don't think it was meant to be.
              Too much happening between you and me.
                Something tells me to slow down,
                  but I can't just stop on this merry-go-round.
                  Don't know where to begin,
                    are you still my friend?
                      Irritated by the silence,
                        in my mind trying to stop the violence.
                        Didn't look your way that day,
                          zoomed in front of you any way
                          Killed the hope for tomorrow,
                            stilled the wings and caused sorrow.
                            Never to be as you once was,
                              never to go home and be with your love.
                              I never meant to make you cry,
                                I never meant to take you from the sky,
                                I never meant "to kill a butterfly."

RW

# LEAVE LOVE MAKING IN THE BEDROOM

Leave love making in the bedroom
Swoon me and contour me
To yours
My nose is spread open
Breathing the aroma
Of love in the air
And when it's all over
And the mist of compassion and thrashing
Grabbing and tugging the pillows
Watching feathers sway from the air
Until it has settled on the bed sheets
The tears of love disintegrate from my face
We left everything the way it was
And then we leave what we felt
In the bedroom

# MY VALENTINE

My love is sweet; my love is kind, especially for you, my Valentine… I could love you true, through and through. So, I thank you now and kiss your hand… I want you, my dearest, to understand… that you make my world a better place… Hmm, to put my lips upon your face… I would tell you things, filled with love, laughter and diamond rings… See how I can dream of the wildest things? But, from my heart to yours, I give you this… a glance of love with a distant kiss… So, take it now and hold it close… 'cause you're the girl I love the most. Happy Valentine's Day!!

RW

# DON'T WANT ANOTHER LOVE WASTED

I don't want another love wasted
Tired of barren grounds
Gravel for mass affection
This one and the next one
Never show their appreciation
Fallen wings and failing dreams
I can't seem to stay connected
Oblivious
Forget my very existence
Then reaching back to your remembrance
Time is gone and the seasons have changed
My last name will still remain the same
I wait for the next season
A new fall color or a new flower breeding
Giving this newness a chance
Hoping for a future glance
I roll around in this new love I found
Hoping it's King Lover I crown
I don't want another love wasted
So I'll wait and
Hold hard to the arms I'm lying in
I watch the clock and hope that time moves on
Hoping I'm not stuck singing the same wretched song
Singing, I don't want another love wasted

# THE GAME

As I look through my window pane,
I often wonder who's to blame for
brokenhearted lovers in the game.
I never wanted to play, never wanted to stay,
too many games, and too much to pay.
Never a beginning and never an end,
never a warning, and you'll never be friends.
We are all guilty of the lie, all guilty of the "why,"
when we knew from the start it would end in goodbye.

RW

# MY FIRST LOVE

It's been forever since we played,
  forever since we moved in tune,
    but we played today in this month of June.

  The rhythm of your bounce,
    the way you feel in my hands,
      would make any true playa understand.

    I know it was me who turned my back,
      never tried again to get on track.
        Believed a lie, when I knew what was true
          Should have taken you all the way to Europe, boo.

      Many good times we shared under the sun,
        Two to four hours a day.
          Yeah, we had a good run.

        Some days were good,
          and some days were bad
            But I would never change the times we had.

          I have missed your touch,
            the way you kissed my game.
              I was very blessed, and I know you felt the same.

I have waited a long time to feel you again,
  and after today,
    you showed me we are still friends.

    So I will always love you,
      always kiss you goodnight.

      Because you were my first love,
        and I took you for granted,
          the parks, the gyms, you had me enchanted.

        But I was young, and you understood.
          I had to play all day and hard to get real good.

        But you travel through time and space
          and you never change your face,
            Only the rhythm of the pace

          I love you… BASKETBALL

# FROM THE MOUNTAIN TOP

I look at my phone
And shake my head
They are all the same
We've said it time and time again
I stand back and watch it
Start on the mountain top
Then little by little
Vitality starts to drop
What happened to the liveliness
That made me priority
What happened to the shimmering life
Of nostalgia when you missed me
It left just like I knew
They are all the same
So common
So true
There should be one
That beats all the odds
The one that's truly unique
The one that can truly love me
Would I open my eyes to be surprised
Or will I cast him into the streets
And pretend a mirage
And say he is just the same
The same as them all
From the mountain top they all eventually fall

# WHEN I AM OLD

Lifestyles of the young and active
And preconditioned arrangements
Have kept you from claiming me
You're neither here nor there
But you are everywhere
In and out of society
I must move on and I must look on
Because you will not come home
Across the world, just passing by
In lovers' arms you will always roam
I cannot fit
I must admit
However, I feel your love
One lifetime with you is all I ask
Amongst several of them
When you have settled
And your arrangement has mellowed
Please come look for me
The love I have for you now
Is still alive and will continue stirring within me
When I am old
And if beauty has not left
And my body is fit with health
If I am still admired with fire in your eyes
Like a doe's eyes in surprise I melt
When I am old come look for me
Tell me all the adventures you encountered
The interesting people you got to know
And the ones you fell in love with
When I am old, settled, and waiting
For a pep and spring of life
Come look for me, I'll be ready
To live young and love senseless nights

# BLACK ACHES

I feel the extraordinary woman who hurts
Her stomach hurts, her sleep interrupts
In her veins it's nothing like crimson red
But blackness instead
She feels a whirlwind of disbelief
When what she believed
Was never meant to be
Her nails are brittle
She's gained a few pounds
Nothing to stir up her beauty inside
Her smile's turned upside down
Drained in regrets
Saying she should have never did that
She holds herself in contention
Razor sharp and depletion
Extraordinary woman
Just the same as every woman
When her heart fails and longs for what matters

# EYES WITHOUT A FACE

Backs turned, times
changed in the blink of
an eye.
Love turned into a heady
wine, left untouched.
Eyes without a face,
no tears to wipe.
What can we do?
Don't want to lose you.
Summer on the rise,
living in the moment
of the passion.
Can you see me… still?
Wandering thoughts
cloud my memory.
Numbness takes my mind,
no words on the page,
so I paraphrase.
A silent prayer for my friend,
hoping to heal from within.
Can't see beyond my cloud,
eyes without a face.

# CAPTURING THE MOMENT

Same black silhouette from the corner of the Manhattan Club
Same black silhouette that lies on the right side of my bed
If I was an artist, I'd replicate the finest beast lying there
Framed in the aftermist of sex
The weather man said it should be sixty percent chance of rain
So the thunder ripples the sky and the rain falls while it prances on my window
Then the essence of sex
Beautified my room
"Till the End of Time" playing on the radio
Hands over his face while one leg, bent, sways
Fighting with weak strength insomnia
He shakes himself to say,
"I'll call you later"

# FAUCET

Drip drop, drip drop…
my love don't stop…
You tightened my love by
turning it tight, but
it won't stop running
cause you left my sight.
I let you turn the handle
and trusted your heart,
but somehow it stripped, and now
it's tearing apart.
I don't want this to happen, not here,
not now, because all of this time
I just wanted to know how…
how I could give you this faucet
and let you twist it around…
turn it on and off and upside down.
Drip drop, drip drop…
my love don't stop…
You loosened my love and
some leaked out.
Now it's flowing from the faucet.
What's this all about?
It's about flowing from this faucet
smooth and slow.
I just wanted you to see, I just wanted you
to know.
Drip drop, drip drop…
My love don't stop…

RW

# I MISS YOU

To indulge in the sweetness
And to wrap my fingers in your nappy-dreaded hair
Tangled in my feet
I stop and just stare
I won't say I love you baby
I'll just say I miss you

# MY ROSE

I have seen her in my garden.
She stands so long and grows.
She blooms with a smile
and a pleasant smell
It's where I like to go.
When the world shuts me down
and all I can do is worry,
she lifts me up with her majestic
presence and I'm thankful in a hurry.
I never want to leave her alone;
just always by her side.
She needs my love and affection,
to help water her soul and mine.
She is my Egyptian flower,
and I her warrior forever.
We will always be as one,
as sure as we are together.

# EYE OF THE STORM

My internal organs
Don't know what to do
An earthquake has erupted
I quiver and shake
From the devastation
I don't know whether to fight
Or to pull him closer
The aftershock is not like any other
But like the soothing eye of a storm
That lasts longer than a moment in time
In his eyes is passion
And fire
Rage and love
I embrace the storm
I fight the storm
And then embrace the love
And peace that succumbs
His passion
I marvel
As I rest and wait
And pull all the bells and whistles
For one more upheaval

# NOT STRONG ENOUGH

Not strong enough to take the blow.
Not strong enough because of my ego.
Not strong enough to take it all in stride.
Not strong enough because of my pride.
Not strong enough to handle your cries.
Maybe not strong enough in between your thighs.
Not strong enough to be your friend.
Not strong enough to lift myself up again.
Not strong enough to be jealous and keep score.
Not strong enough to hang around anymore.
Not strong enough to hide the hurt.
Not strong enough and I feel like dirt.
Not strong enough to hide the tears.
Not strong enough after all these years.
NOT STRONG ENOUGH!

# HOW COULD YOU

How could you
Knowing my love
Was as deep as space
How could you
When all I did
Was love you
Entirely
How could you
Display my affections
And wreck them with
Heartless, thoughtless,
Careless collections
Of actions
I was a fool
To think that love
Gains respect
You have changed my mind
Love precedes hurt
How could I love again?
How could I give myself again?
How can I feel again?
An EKG reading would be able to tell
That my heart is afloat and near death
I lie in my bed with my pillow soaked
God please revive me
Just one grain of hope
That I can survive this
I can get by this
Healing, do not flee me

# I WILL NO LONGER SERVE

I will no longer serve…
Because it hurts my heart to see you
struggling with your way of doing things.
You say one thing and do another.
Contradiction is your teacher now.
Your thoughts and feelings betray you.
As I sit and ponder what might have
been. I struggle to free my heart from
your love that caught and chained me.
My very life was in your keeping.
I will no longer serve
because the loneliness is unbearable.
Forgetfulness is your answer when it
comes to me and remembrance
when there is a need. So quick to your
side I come running with a passion,
only to be cast aside like an old wash rag
once it's served its purpose.
I will no longer serve…
Because I have a choice, just as you do
for someone special, who will make me feel special.
Far from your love I shall flee,
far from your touch and your emotions.
I will no longer serve
because in order to live again, my love for
you must die. So I will kill it for
my own existence. I feel selfish for these
actions, and it hurts me so. But I can
no longer serve a love that has betrayed me.
My emotions escape me.
I will no longer serve.
This is the end of my pain,
my favors, my time, my constant love
that I kept close to my heart.
Please understand my path, for
it was already written for me as it was for you.
You betray me with an eternal kiss
and thus have wasted my love and my heart.
I WILL NO LONGER SERVE!

RW

# I RUN FROM LOVE

I run from love
Not because I've been so deeply hurt
Or that he left me
For the female in the tight knit skirt
It's not because he lied or belittled me
It's not because he got caught cheating
It's not because he wanted someone better
Or supposedly prettier
It's not because he would never say
That he loved me because he was
Busy loving somebody else
It's not that he hurt me so bad
Or that he left me standing in the rain
And left me holding a whole horde of pain
I run from love and despise love so
I run from love because my desperation
To find my equal
To find a true soulish tie, weaved and wrapped around my soul
One who will know and understand me
My ins and outs
Who I am
Never skipping a beat
With one heartbeat and one soul
With an assurance
That no one else is meant to be
Except you and me

And when we stand before God he wouldn't see
Me as an individual but the other part of himself
That was made exactly for me
So for the ones I meet while I am trying to find
The one created that God took time
To perfect
I'm not worried about you not calling me
I'm not worried about you cheating on me
I'm just weaving you out
I'm just feeling my way
Waiting for
The moment when I look
The One in the eyes
At the very moment time stops
And beyond doubt
I can finally, finally, finally—genuinely say, "I Love You!"

# ADDICTED TO ONE SIDE OF THE BED

Addicted to one side of the bed.
Where you used to lay your head.
The smell of your hair still fills the air.
Tossing and turning, can't sleep.
Spine twisted,
neck cracked,
finally all the way down my back.
Each night is a blur as I sit on a four- to six-hour time clock,
tick tock, tick tock.
Can't get right,
it's another night…
Of tossing and turning. Waking up
on one side of the bed.
Tired of my life strains and dealing with
the pains of losing another love.
Selfish in my ploy to make her love me more, but that was not
the case, that was not my chore.
Now we wait only time will tell, but
I have erased all of the images from my chip,
and all the memories I can skip.
Still dealing with sharp wounds that scratch my heart,
wanting the healing to finally start.
So until I can find a way to have peace inside my head,
I will stay addicted to one side of the bed.

RW

# IT'S A RAINY DAY

Just when you think you're the only one
Someone else comes floating from up above
You see I feel this rainy weather too
It's hitting me so good
Depression eating me up
Gallon-sized tears swelling up
Trying to maintain and be professional
Wondering what in my life has value besides the natural things
And why those important to me are so far from me
Wondering if those close to me
Are really holding up their authenticity
I think too much
And then I drink too much
To drown away what's eating away at me.
Wanting to throw my love on someone on a one-night flight
But at the same time, hyping my conscious that I'm all right
I do enjoy being single sometimes
I mostly don't want to be anybody's property
I just want someone to please me
Hold me all night and follow me in my dreams
But because of a substandard history, I just can't let that be
Not now…
Love doesn't remain the same
Love never fails to change
Just like adding too much water to dilute it
Somehow I just knew it
It loses its flavor
It loses its savor
What in the hell must I do
To get over this fever
This fever of depression
Yes, I feel the one I'm responding to
This weather can make any one of us feel so damn blue.
But I'll be okay
I'll keep pressing on
Self therapeutics—singing and feeling new lively songs
New songs and new memories
That will make this day just another rainy day
For tomorrow we'll be just fine

# THESE THREE WORDS

These Three Words I speak to you.
These Three Words are tried and true.
Never will they lie to you and
never will they take from you.
Always behind you.
Always in front of you.
Always wanting you and always
needing you.
These words have raised many.
These words have praised plenty.
I have sacrificed myself for this.
I have prayed and prayed for your kiss.
These Three Words, powerful are they.
These Three Words will never stray.
Only spoken at the moment of truth,
only meant just for you.
These Three Words are forever hers.
These Three Words… "I LOVE YOU."

RW

# SO GOOD

That was so good
My hands still shake
That was so good
My knees are still weak
That was so good
My feet are still curled
That was so good
I'm still in the zone
That was so good
I can't think straight
That was so good
I can't concentrate
That was so good
I'm having flashbacks
That was so good
Goosebumps up and down
My back
That was so good
I want it again
Come one more time
One more time
To feel like this again

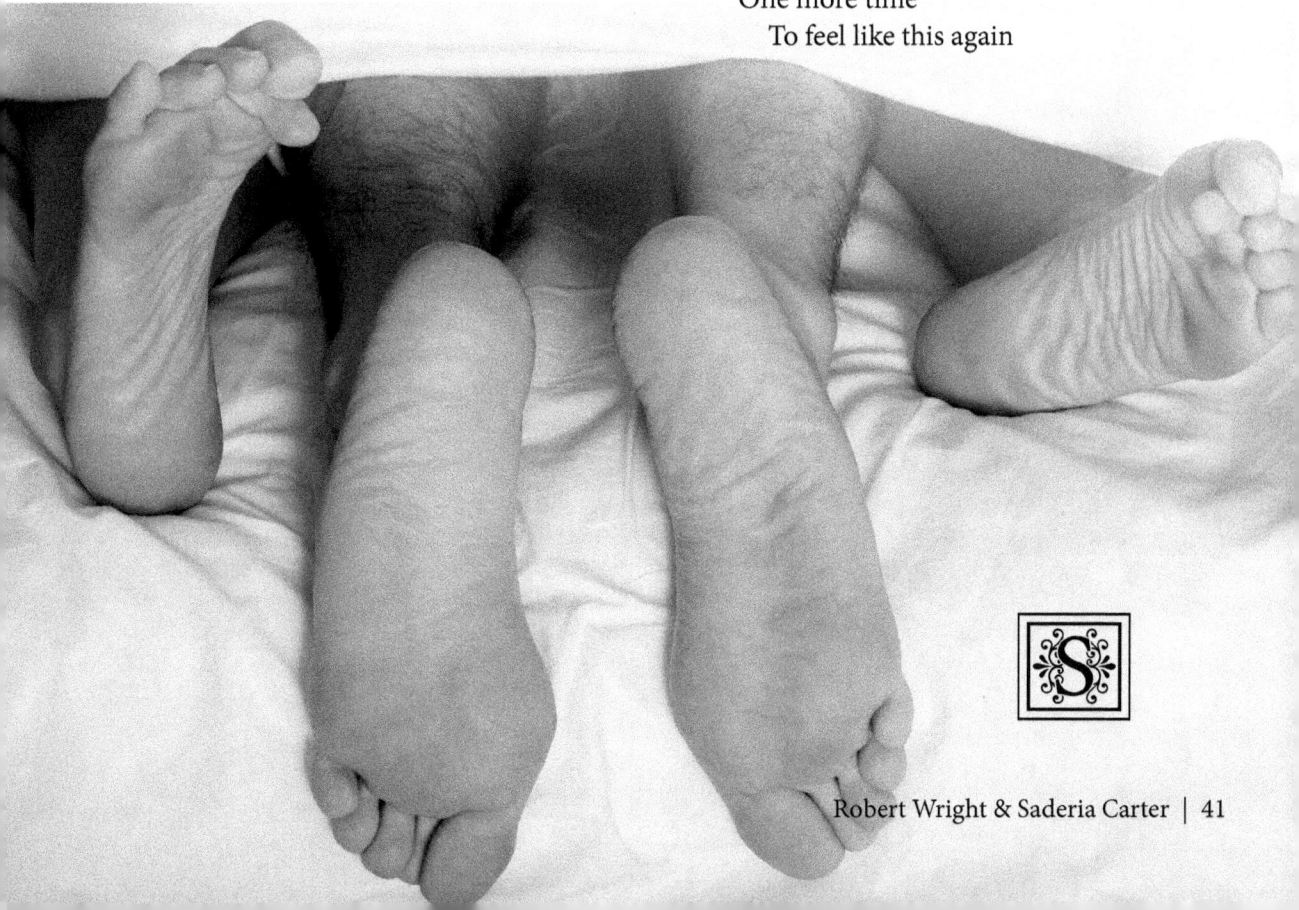

# MISSED KISSES

Missed kisses on my pillow,
fallen from my mind like a dream.
The touch of her lips covered
my smile. It was cool to have
them there.
And her smile was my prize
when I looked into her eyes.
I have missed those kisses
and sometimes the wishes,
of happiness.
Missed kisses on my heart,
because inside myself, forgiveness
has to start…
I love her more, and the struggle begins.
In life no one wins… only missed kisses.

RW

# NO FAIRYTALES HERE

I told God to take it back
The prayer that I once prayed
Sleepy dreams
And hopefulness
Of meeting my soul mate
A fairytale reality
It wasn't meant to be
A molded figure
Created
Just for me
I waited for many years
Tapping my fingers against the table
Watching my wrist
Wondering if God
Is really able
My patience was worn
Settled
And dreaded with impatience
Anxiousness riding me
In my mind
Continual reminiscence
Now my dream has died
The hope light within has blown out
For I will never know a fairytale
What Cinderella and the Prince

Is really all about
I have no hope
I am immune
Because of all the things
I went through
So now, God, I take it back
The prayer I prayed to you
I will be alone
And peruse along the way
Maybe a mere glimpse of
The prayer I prayed
Will surface one day
But I fear I have nothing
To give if a soul mate
Finally appeared
For my hasty decisions
Have wounded my heart
And it has wounded my visional appeal
So, God, just take it back
I am no gift
To anyone you have made
Singleness is me
Just hopeless
For the rest of infinity

# A PRAYER FLUNG
# UP TO HEAVEN

A prayer flung up to heaven one day
I said, Lord, why does my heart long so
For the love of an African Prince
Who has forgotten me
Why should my heart faint
When his eyes can no longer
Soar deeply into mine
And can no longer
Enter into my soul
To be the whole universe with me
Why should I be troubled
When you have saved me
From trouble
From a future heart failure
That would befall my entire intelligence
And crazy I would be
Mentally losing
Thank you, Lord, that I feel not free
But I am free

# STEP OFF

I don't have time for this
Do I love or am I confused
About the heaviness that contemplates
    My heart, my mind, and wonder if my soul
    Should be twisted with yours
    I never saw a glimmer of light
        And gave up on the idea
        And said that there is no light
        At the end of the tunnel
            So I rumble on and play
            As if I will never win anyway
            So, love, do not stare me in the face now
                I've long given up
                I dismiss my ever knowing you
                Affections and regrets
                    Tears flowing down
                    Why now do you shake my foundation
                    Forcing me to look and stare you head on
                        Like an unforeseen revelation
                        I'm uncomfortable with this monkey on my back
                        I'd rather see you in a distance
                            And only feel the tip of your wings
                            Than to fly in the sunlight with you
                            Fear is my shield and the protector of heart
                                So, love, step off!

# THE NEXT BEST THING

When the time comes
When you've faced
A strong wind
You stop fighting to turn
And go in the flow of it
Your love is lost
And your friends have swayed
And your happy face
Is now a dull blade
Instead of fighting for what you once loved
And instead of caring too much
To compel a better outcome
You just stand in the wind and
Let the force move you
To the next best thing

# THE SUN AND MIDNIGHT

I'm going to hold you
And rock you like the midnight
Until morning seeps into the day
You can't stop the sun from warming you
As it caresses your being
The lightness of the morning
Wakes you up and then you are ready
The planets align
When you're around
And it feels like the world stops rotating
When your face finally comes around the corner
And reveals a hint of excitement
The time passes but seems like an enjoyable eternity
The sun starts to rise
In my being
And the light of the sun illuminates
A fascinating moment in my existence
The sun starts to dim as
The night makes its way
A full moon graces the sky
And settles as I descend to sleep

# DO YOU THINK OF ME

Voice as deep as the waves
Are you Vin Diesel's brother
My lover
So hard to forget
Why do I give in and why can't I
Completely bury my memory of you
Knowing we can't mix
Spaces in my life are so incompetent
The things you did inspired me
Always wanting me to do and be better
You motivated and convinced me that the world
was completely mine.
I was your queen, you were proud of me, and I was your pride.
We fought and we loved
We screamed and we hugged
I scroll down my phone often
Seeing your number
I wonder
What are you doing
And do you still think about me?

# TIMID SUMMER

I just can't wait for the summer time
When the winter chills pass on by
High expectation with newness
To breath
Heart aches the winter brought
I'm picking them with tweeze
Unwrapping myself out of the cloak
Of disbelief
Taking off the pain and misery
Slipping on something short and sleazy
Laying back while the sun heals me
Smile on my face
Nothing can take it away
Summer time breeze
Making it a feel-good day
I'm watching and waiting
For the seasons to change
Holding my breath for the
Timid summer days

# TOMORROW IS
# NOT PROMISED

I love you right now
I love you today
But I cannot promise
That I will love you always
It was you I decided to love
But now I must let it die
Or else it will kill me
And take the rest of my life

# TODAY, TOMORROW, AND THE DAY AFTER

Today, can I see you?
It's been some time
Since I last saw you
Seems like I see you
In a 3-D visual effect
Brown and glowing complexion
And shimmering eyes like tears glaring back
Makes me want to come see you tomorrow
Seems like there's something to you glorified
Your beauty must have magnified
A thousand times
What did you do to make me
Want to
Come back the day after that
I cannot object
That I've fallen
Twisted and locked in your garden
There is no mistake
That I want to spend the remnants of today
Tomorrow and the day after
Seeing you, lying next to you
The day after and the day after—infinite…

# TRAVELING TO HARTFORD

I met him in cyber
Love waves taking me higher
As I imagine him
With the baggy jeans
Dropped at the waistline
Tight braids straight back
Blingin' while he's chillin'
Distance and too many miles
For my mind to travel wishing
I could just chill
With him and talk to him
While the sky is blue
Till the sky is pitch-black
A bottle of his favorite
While we laugh just to be laughing
When nothing is funny
Goose bumps manifest themselves
Just because I'm glad to be here
With him
Reaching out as I rub my fingertips across
His tight braids
And then finally caressing him
And smoothing my lips to his cheeks
While the sky is blue
Till the sky is pitch-black
Then making love and spending time
While the sun is pushing up
And the moon is pushing back
The distance and the miles
Rewind
I'm back to the reality that
My nonfictional love
Is really only a click away

# UNSPOKEN WORDS

Knowing the situation
Is as tight
As my legs crossed
When dirty words
Fill my ears
My heart flutters
When your arms are
Wrapped around my flesh
Wetness on my toes
Wetness on my lips
Wetness on my figure tips
Wetness where people can't see
I won't say I love you
But I'll just say I miss you
To my surprise
You are not
Like another
Further wishes
For you to stay
But it's just business
That's what we say
No words allowed
To express how we truly feel
The choices we made
Could take a toll
But still…

# WAKING UP…

I wanna wake up with locks laying across my face
I wanna wake up feeling your breath waving across my ears
I wanna wake up with your back pressed against my chest
I wanna wake up with your secret parts mashed against my hinder parts
I wanna wake up with your legs tangled in mine like vines
I wanna wake up with the heels of your feet resting on the tip of my toes

     Moans in my ears, palms rolling down my arm
     Rolling around
     Lips to my lips
     Hands on my ass
     Legs tangled in mine like vines
     Right leg to your left
     Morning dew is our residue
     The day after, the morning after
     Waking up.

# WHAT I WANT

You need to understand that he is not your man
So you can't pretend and play imaginary accommodation
For the sake of a mentality to create a happy depiction
When the empathy of your spirit needs to be shown
A little bit more love and compassion
Tell it to your hormones when you're alone
That you are fine and you don't need anyone
But you do need someone to love and hold
For as long as you want
And then to tell him to go home
When you look in his eyes and you caress in his arms
Look at the clock it's time for him to bounce
You scream inside and you wonder why such perfection
Instantly, you remember you're not his
And he's not yours
And you remember the frozen picture
Of the depiction of a picture of a moment of happiness
Is now savored away
By the tears in your soul
That didn't want to let him go
You just want one thing
For the sake of a happy depiction
When the empathy of your spirit needs to be shown
A little more love and compassion
For as long as you want
And then to tell him to go home.
What more can you ask for
What more can you do
But chew on this salt-less life
When everything but everything can happen
You don't ask for much
You just want one thing
And that's to get what you want
And then to tell him to go home.

# YELLOW PLUMS

Escaping iron fist
And hiding the stitches
She gathered her children
And left
She has family
To hide away in refuge they can temporarily provide
She wipes her tears and she gathers her pride
And finds a way to survive
Now on her own she finds her way
She finds a place
A little four-room white house—so small
There's a tree filled with yellow plums
On the west side of the house
Tons of plums rotten on the ground
On the tree so small but plump and round
Everyday struggle to struggle
Cold water to busted windows
Two adolescent children
And single parenting obstacles
Every year the plums return
Until one day the tree is gone
Seems that when the tree
Was hemmed up
We moved on to a better life.

# A FOOL'S HEART

How does it feel to smash a champagne glass against the wall?
Not even deep down inside I knew I could never really have it all
Shattering glass won't make the pain erase
Watching a movie to get lost in someone else's fantasy
It's like window shopping on Park Avenue
I can try it on
Can't buy this so now what am I to do?
It's hurting so deep that I can't be next to you
Every day, like revenue
Hands in my pocket
Not pulling nothing out
How to get over loving you—I can't figure this shit out
It's like rocking somebody else's boat on borrowed time
How in the hell are they going to have what I seasoned all this while
I know an end shall come to pass
Watching the sand fall through an hour glass
I'm picking up the glass scattered on the floor
Felt like smashing another one against the door
But broken glass won't change a thing
My heart and mind tell me I'll never get that diamond ring
Not even a promise
Not even a friends for life through the stormy weather
In the valley on the mountain top, not even when the rain drops
I'm feeling you, but I know there's nothing I can do
But to enjoy the ride until my time is due
I'm holding you until the time fades away
Watching the champagne glass, in reverse, as though it was never shattered
Knowing someday its future is inevitable

# SHADE TREE NIGGA

You shade tree nigga.
You are a disgrace.
You kill your own brother,
and "he" laughs in your face.
"He" silently steals your bread.
"He" will enslave you again too.
You will never see it coming,
unless you read a book or two.
Why must we struggle on a daily basis?
Why can't we all be friends?
See, you just living foul and "you"
going to kill hope again.
Don't you see it's all done with smoke and mirrors?
A Hollywood scene written in the dark.
I know who's playing the role of the
shade tree part.
If only I could turn back the hands of time.
I would ask God to not make wrong, but only make right.
I know that wouldn't have worked, because God wanted us
to fight.
Fight for a love that could only be true.
Fight for the love that was built in you.
So my friend I implore you to change your ways.
We didn't ask to be immortal enemies of each other.
I didn't want to kill my soul. I just wanted you to be
my brother.
See I used to be like you.
Tattle tale on a friend or two, and tap dancing
for the man with the gun in my hand.
I know now it was just a bitter lie, and why I pulled the trigga.
See I used to be like you. A shade tree nigga.

RW

# BOULE NIGGA

Let's see; where do I start?
Where black people broke my heart.
Sold into slavery by my very own,
the watchdog cowards of the
British throne.
So, now we are here in the twenty-first century.
The Hollywood niggas still slaves to history.
You made us love your wealth,
and still hate ourselves.
For what? The money and the power?
House niggas still telling on field niggas.
You might as well have pulled the trigga.
You have already sold your life to the boule.
So, I feel sorrow for you and your wicked ways.
Collecting souls by your homosexual ways,
will get you tossed in the lake of fire, one of these
days.
Repent, my brothers, to the one who sits on the most high,
or face his wrath and surely die.
I can't believe you sold me out once again,
believing you were my brother to the very end.
Most people will not be able to conceive that
the watchdog association of the NAACP,
was started by two white men,
to organize our so-called sin.
Reporting to the white satanic masters who run amuck,
who shall doom the world, and still call you schmuck?
You two-faced, back-stabbing, sell-out gold digga,
I should have hanged you myself, you boule nigga.

RW

# THE INTERVIEW

"You can take an application, but you can't have the job."
"Yeah, we have a quota we have to maintain."
"So what's your nationality, color, religion,
and your name?"
"Please don't take this the wrong way, but you
don't have what we are looking for, we knew this
about you the moment you came through the door."
"But I would like to thank you for stopping by.
I really enjoyed your conversation, even though
under that suit I could feel your frustration."
"In order to get a good job with us
you need to come through the back door,
and keep a low profile if you want us to like
you more."
"Quickly, let's shake hands so others
can see I was polite. Then I can wish you good
luck as you walk out of my sight."

RW

# HE HATE ME

Here we go again;
you trying to classify me
because of the color of my skin.
You made me hate my origin;
you made me love your sin.
You broke my ways, my spirit,
even tore my skin.
You changed my name,
my life, and even took my children,
plus my wife.
My brother sold me off for
some pocket change.
Now you look at me like I'm something
strange?
I can't stand to look at my brother anymore
because I hate myself for being poor.
I'm pretty sure he feels the same
because we got robbed and "you" are to
blame!
Now I'm 10,000-plus miles away from home.
Shipped to North America, shackled to the bone.
He hates me, and for the life of me,
I don't know why.
I didn't ask to be "taken" here,
and the rest of us you told a lie.
And after 400 years of this filth and stench,

our minds are still slaves under Willie Lynch.
"The Making of a Slave" was taught to every
plantation owner in the South,
and they claimed to be Christians; what's that
all about?
Forgive me, my brother, for what I have done,
but forgive the masters? It's gonna be a huge one.
The differences they created between you and me
were color, fear, trust and envy.
Age was another factor that played a role,
and the children so young were raped and stole.
They took the strongest amongst us and
ripped him apart, so the women would fear
them and raise her child to be smart.
Smart enough to not resist, and
become deadweight.
Thus, the mother was kept in check, and her son
in a weak state.
A boy now a man, and a stranger
in a new land.
Kept from knowledge of self and a good life.
Humanity has failed us, in the back with a knife.
I implore you, my friend, to educate yourself,
because slavery has no color,
and it will repeat itself.

RW

# GENOCIDE

I thought my big brother was supposed to be there in strife,
instead it was murder throughout history of human life.
First, he bribed my neighbors because he knew they were greedy and vain.
Then the perils of famine, war, and disease had a new name.
He took the children from mother nature, and physically damaged
their anatomy.
Now they can't have children, and in the Bible, that's blasphemy.
For whom so ever damages these pure of heart, shall not see
heaven, but hell is a good start.
Now I see the true face of Satan with his treachery and disguise.
His deep hatred of love, self, and others, but soon he will meet his demise.
Big brother has always had a plan to exterminate
parts of the human race.
I just can't believe he almost accomplished it right here in our face.
The trick sold to society was that it was doing a service for good.
So, they mandated some policies and laws, then called it "Planned Parenthood."
I never thought of it this way; I might as well be laying in a tomb
because the toughest place to survive is in a mother's womb.
"The choice" you make should be whether to have intercourse at all
because once you lay ground work, you have made that final call.
No one knows that they tried to pass a law that if you had
a child and were poor, abortion was the last straw.
They covered it up and warehoused it in politics,
called our children feebleminded and labeled it eugenics.
Yeah, Planned Parenthood and abortion go hand in hand.
They have killed the kindness of humanity and the true nature of man.
I will leave you with this and I hope you can relate.
Love your neighbor and thyself, and pray it's not too late.

RW

# DIE FOR FREEDOM

See, I have always died for freedom.
Whether it be a crack of the whip
or some old stupid shit.
No, you won't catch me running from trouble,
instead you will see me up in the rubble.
I don't like to be shackled or chained in color.
Let me be, or you will see the true me!
See, YOU don't want to talk about the 22 million
who died in bravery.
YOU sweep it under the rug, and just call it slavery.
I'm a product of mixture, and the last known survivor
of the so-called negro you refuse to hire.
The time is short, and the day will come.
Soon it will be YOU under the gun.
No, I'm not going to shoot YOU.
I will let you play out your role
because where I will be, you sure cannot go.
Beat me, chain me, chase me, and kill me.
That is all you seek.
Pitiful because you cannot defeat the meek.
I will die for my right as a human being.
I will die for my family whom I love.
I will die for YOU and your ignorant ways,
and finally, but surely, I will die for FREEDOM!

RW

# THE SOUND OF FREEDOM

The sound of freedom rang through my walls.
I thought of the many men, women, and children
who have died for it all.
My heart rings out in doubt.
We are not yet free.
Some of us are still sold to the highest bidder.
Most of us still like the word nigger.
The shots of glory shine bright in the air
as the nation is sold right from beneath
our chairs. "Made in China."
You don't know; you better read the inscription.
Loud thunder cracks and booms from the celebration,
hand cuffs locked, and shots fired without hesitation.
I'm trying to figure out why you hate me so.
You are supposed to be my bro.
No more plantations, but another field of labor
called a job, or just over broke.
When will we be free? I'm tired and thirsty.
I need a place to lay my burden. I hear the sound of
freedom just over the horizon. I'm not going to give in,
and if you think I will, then think again.
"Endurance and patience," my father once said,
"Are what you need to do before you rest your head."
The sound of freedom rings in my heart and soul.
I want YOU to listen, so one day you will know.
Follow the sound of freedom, and to heaven you shall go.

RW

# AWAKE WHILE SLEEPING

It was the dream that made me think
about my life, about this link.
I was in a reality all my own.
I sat quietly on my thrown.
King of none but friend to many;
enemies come, I don't need any.
My reality seems surreal
because I'm controlled by its appeal.
Now the only time I am free
is when I'm asleep inside of me.
There I am free from hate, jealousy, and lies,
and anything else humanity can surmise.
If we could somehow figure out this state,
then the world would be a better place.
So, I'm stuck in peril,
and I pray for safekeeping,
while I live this life awake while sleeping.

RW

# FABRIC

If a man doesn't compliment me
And notice my halo when I walk into a room
If he doesn't respect me
Or add value to me
He is like a plaid shirt or a woolen suite
Clashing with my fine silk
If a woman accepts the man
Who dismisses her intelligence
While he flips open her legs to only admire what's between
And calls her appellations
Unacceptable
She has decreased her own value
And ruined her own fabric

# LOVE, LIFE, MELISSA

Why you wanna keep your child?
Do you love
Or do you feel pressure?
Pressure from the heavens
Or pressure from the fella
Pressure from the family
Friends
Or pressure from your belly
The choice is great
Right choice
Wrong choice
A decision has got to be made
Tick tock
Time ticks
And people who know you

Wait
A waiting room
Of people
Waiting on a verdict
Pro-life or pro-choice
Pro-live or pro-die
Whose future?
Your future or its future?
Hard future or a grateful future?
So many things to consider
So little time
What will you do?

# REBEL DOVE

Life took away the innocence
She was a rare flower
A solemn dove
Sweet as nectar
She can't remember her life as it was
Now she's rebel bad
Cigarette in her hand
She's young but her skin
Has no elasticity
Heart failure
Leaves no room
For love to live freely
Her rareness is now the norm
Her innocence
Scared and scorned
The little girl
A flown away dove

# SEARCHING FOR PEACE

How can you possibly understand
Where I've been and what I have to do right now?
The hardest thing to look head on
I ride by
And I drive by looking for
The right answers to these questions
I'm boggled down
And I'm stressed to all ends
What have I gotten myself into?
They say to talk to those you love
They say to write your pros and cons
But still I have no peace
I just want to go in reverse
And prevent this occurrence
To never have occurred
The priests are gone and no one is around
I sit in the parking lot thinking aloud
Then thinking silently to myself
And then looking up toward heaven
What should I do?
No one knows what I must feel
To wonder whether or not
If I want another child
I can't go in
I can't let go of this child inside
This child is mine
I'm glad to have a choice
The people that surround me in personal life
Are people I can trust
They will hold my hand
Regardless of my choice
Love goes a long way
I have lots of love to give
Nine months plus many years of life
My choice, it's life—my life

# THAT BIRD IS DEAD

I heard the birds singing
They flocked together in one unison family
Too bad and so sad
That one would go missing
I thought it would be for fun
I thought I'd be a man
Just shoot some pellets
Into the air
Bang once
Bang twice
Nothing but flocking into the sky
Bang three times
Bang four
Something happened
I was not ready for
I shot that bird
I shot him dead
It crushed all the feeling I had
I'm supposed to feel different
Proud and swollen
At my chest
Feeling like a man
But I didn't and felt lousy instead
That bird is dead
That bird is gone
Never will I take a life
For fun again

# GOD'S LOVE FOR SATAN

You loved me once, before time itself,
before all of the rest.
Now, you choose your ego from
your chest.
All of eternity, I have given to you,
and all of my love I have anew.
Now all that I do is entertain your misery,
throughout all the centuries I've grown weary.
Because of your actions you are forlorn as you could ever be,
and you shall have your place far away from me.
What hurts me so is that we will never know
how much love you didn't show.

# SATAN'S WILL

You are my father and my friend.
Why don't you let me live again?
You have shown me much about the will of love,
but now I love only me instead of you from above.
I cannot be what you want me to be;
I can only be what you designed for me.
So, I will destroy all that you love,
and all that I love too.
So I can be an equal in this game with you.
I know you will not stop me,
and I know I will not win,
but I just want to be something special,
something like a friend.
You loved me once upon a time.
Now your love for me will never be mine.
I'm fine with that because I'm beautiful alone.
In fact, I'm happy upon my throne.
I will say this, my father,
you have given me very much.
I will always answer to you,
for you I cannot touch.
You clever one, you tricked me,
the greatest trickster of all, by having
your favorite son born, it was the writing
on the wall.
So now I'm jealous with envy,
hate, disgust and all.
I will destroy mankind forever,
and die in the final fall.

RW

# FREEDOM OF THE CAGED BIRD

I see a caged bird
Sitting at a crossroad
Waiting for a passing stranger
To set him free
The caged bird
Sits and waits
While he dreams for
Life to finally catch up with him
Sometimes too far ahead of itself
He finds himself in snared situations
So now he waits for a passing stranger
To set him free
In the glimmer of light
Down the dusty road quite a ways
Slowly creeps to his presence
Someone with the pass to life
Anticipation overwhelms
And excitement can't be contained
For he knows soon
He will be set free
And then it clouds his mind
How could he thank the
Stranger for unlocking
The doors
Of freedom
The stranger arrives and
Says,
"To thank me
Learn something, grow stronger, and
Try not to get caught again."

# MY FATHER AND MY DAD

Today I thank my heavenly father
for watching over me all night long.
I pray that he can make me just a little stronger.
Strong enough to withstand the
worst amount of pain, so that my
love for life can conquer the strain
of everyday trials that come my way.
Especially the one on Father's Day.
Even though my earthly dad has gone
his way, I can still feel his presence,
until this very day.
Sometimes the past can tell you a lot.
Sometimes it can tell you who you are not.
Thank you, Dad, for giving us your best.
Now you are with your father in eternal rest.
But while you were here you helped spark
my life. You gave me a sense of family that
I want to have someday with a wife.
I know now what I didn't know then—
that you have always loved us, even until the end.
So, today, I honor you and say thanks once again.
Love you, Dad, and thanks for being my friend.

RW

# THE GARDEN

I know now what I should not. They planned
our demise but they forgot.
They know not what they do.
It is in vain that they try to unglue
the fabric of everyone's being.
Slithering below because what was once
is no more. You frighten the children with your
violence and gore.
Your lying tongue betrays
you in the end, and you will burn forever,
forever my friend.
My friend, that's what I thought.
You pretty little liar, look what you brought.
A legacy that will soon be forgotten;
a legacy that is slowly rotting.
I shall look into the face of the ancient one
and know that I am an eternal son.
Thank you, Father, for holding my hand
when I pulled away and became a man.
I am that I am because of you.
And I will always, forever love you true.

RW

# JUST WHAT I NEEDED

What do you know about the world
And what do you know about me
You swing your dreads and you swing
Your body to a rhythmic tune
While you hope for any gloom
To evaporate into oblivion
Right before it sends the sunlight
To exude in the hearts of Jah people
You sing your highs and sometimes your lows
Just so the people in the valley will know
That hope is here
And can be touched
You pump your fist
And you say to stand up
And you say to jam
You say to dance
I obey and feel you
Swinging your body to a rhythmic tune
While I hope for any gloom
To wane away
I whine my waist and I close my eyes
While you take me there
On a faraway island
Yes, way over there
I feel the sun shine away the gloom
And the Rasta leads my heart to peace

# WHEN THE STARS FALL

Where shall you run when the stars fall? Your love for it all
will crumble like dreams with a wrecking ball.
You don't love yourself or even protect yourself.
How can you love someone you have never seen?
How can you trust someone you have never believed?
I ask you again, where shall you run when the stars fall?
Nowhere, I tell you, because you stall.
You have arrived at life's short fate,
hoping and praying it's not too late.
Search your feelings; search for your soul.
You are out of time, and the evil one knows.
Where shall you run when the stars fall?

# LAST NIGHT IN THE BELLY OF THE BEAST

How did I get to such a horrible place?
Sex, lies, and video tape.
I hate what I have become, uncaring to
the world, and no stranger to being numb.
Sold to making money, and bought at a cheap price.
I don't know how I was duped into thinking this was right.
Looking back on yesterday, I was just a teen.
Careless to responsibilities and all sorts of things.
Where's my Walt Disney and my house full of love?
Crushed by drunkenness, and the casual use of drugs.
It was here I must guess that my memories escaped free!
Nightmares cradled and tried to seduce me.
Tortured souls are celebrated here,
and fed lie after lie, until ultimately you die…
I have always known righteousness. I have
always known good—deep down in my soul.
I just forgot that I could…
Could love someone that would love me back.
Could trust someone who could do just that.
Could believe what Jesus said:
"Remember the world hated me first." In spite of the world's dreaded curse.
A prayer in the darkness, answered into the light.
Now I know my Lord and savior, I know him with all my might.
I was not forgotten there, but now I know why he sent me.
I must be a friend to those, even the ones who hate me.
I am the pain that once penetrated my soul, but now
I will get the chance to walk the streets of gold.
No longer will I lie in wait;
no longer will evil rule my fate.
Thank you, Lord, for showing me my sin,
and if you wanted me to do it over, I'd do it again.
Amen

RW

# IS THIS REAL

Finding a glimmer of light
Shadowing a tunnel full of darkness
Through this life
You've concluded that there is no light
To be immune to hopeless thoughts of real and true keenness
You squint your eyes in soft amazement
That after all this time
And after all these battles
After all these tears and wishful years
At the end of your tunnel
is what you dreamed and unrealistic
fantasies happen to be tangible
You reach out as if it was a dream
And then you're blown away by the mere
Realization that
You're awake

# MY FATHER'S PRAYER

The world is my burden; I carry it's torch…
For centuries past, I have sat on heaven's porch,
loving mankind, in spite of how he felt about me.
Loving what was created out of dust and misery.
Freedom of choice and the way you want to live,
but you chose shackles of hatred instead to forgive.
All individual issues will come to an end.
My arms are open to you; my love I will lend.
But you know it is yours to keep—
a gift for you, a gift from me.
When you think your life has passed you by,
remember me, because for you I will not lie.
Have faith in me for I have faith in you.
There's nothing like a father's love;
there's nothing that compares to you.
Remember, I know you better than these;
I have loved you longer than the centuries.
I am the eternal marketer, who answers every call,
so don't hang up now, but give it your all.
My children, how pleased am I to see you grow.
Let's hope that you can one day be free.
Let's hope that all people can truly see
that all it takes is believing in me…

RW

# MY SIN

Bathed in sin…
When will I live again?
Tired of the rusty chains,
that shackle me in pain.
Will I be able to be cured from this insanity?
I close my eyes to think of peace,
and pray to the lord to kill the beast,
that rages inside my weary mind,
who strangles my spirit all the time.
Every day, I wage the war, but somehow
I fall victim to the beast once more.
How can I fight what I cannot see?
I'm down on bended knee.
My struggle, my pain, my win, my loss,
when will it ever change?
One day I shall never be the same.
The plan I now follow shall reign high supreme
for it is "he" who knows about my dream.
It ends now; as shall a "new" begin.
I need you around, my friend.
My life is in your hands now, and I proudly
submit it to thee.
Thank you, thank you for loving me…

RW

# MY FIGHTING MOTHER

Smash, clash, glass breaks
Furniture moving and the walls vibrate
Blood trickling
Tears flowing
There is no love
For the abused woman
No job, no money
He gives her twenty dollars a week to eat
And to feed her children meat
Bologna and potty meat
Wonder bread—and wondering why
A mother is dealing with this bloody crime
Shackled by the black woman's place
To abide
Swallow your pride and stay, they say
Until one day
Her body was tired
Of being torn
Tired of being busted
Tired of the fear
Tired of the tears
Tired of this cage-less prison
She broke loose!

Finally
Fear did not repress her
but fear was suppressed
With proud statue, she said:
I now have a job
I have a life
I have a car and
I am still beautiful
I don't need you
I now have a house
I have my children
I have my dignity and
I have my pride
I don't need you.
The once noticeable scars have faded
Her heart has long been healed
Life is all right
Without the grueling fight
Of the abused woman.

# MY CROSS

Stuck in thought, can't
shake the vault…
of troubled things
in the ring… of life.
When does the real fun start?
When does the fake stuff fall apart?
Tired of working for slave wages;
disgusted by the lines in between the pages.
My life spent sold to the highest bidder.
Everyday feeling punched by the one-hitter-quitter.
Hmph, trying to make it right.
Everyday a different strife.
Got to wait it out a little longer,
till I'm righteous and a little stronger.
So one day I can break my chains
and be glorious in his name.
But right now, it's been ten years
under the shroud of darkness,
looking for my special light, to make
this tribulation go away in his sight.
To my Father, I pray…
Amen

# WAR

God is the door, and Jesus is the key.
Unlock the door, and set yourself free.
Troubled waters running through my hands,
flooding the minds and hearts of the sacred lands.
NOW DO YOU UNDERSTAND?
Diseased souls believe the lie.
Spread by the one who promised your demise.
Killed the innocent and the true blood lines;
tore off the believers from the fruit of the vines.
How much longer must we endure
the world's pains and incurable cures?
Uncontrollably shaking and falling to my knees;
the bombs keep dropping, stripping the earth of her trees.
They kill the flesh and try to take your soul.
But you are God's child, and they will never reach that goal.
For your soul was never yours to keep.
all the tribulations that made you weak
were God's way of testing your spirit.
But many of us don't want to hear it.
So to the depths of Hades, where most will dwell,
right beside Satan himself in the lap of hell.
So you say you will fight for your life. You say you want more.
Then give your life to Jesus, if you want to win this WAR!

RW

# MY GRANDMOTHER'S TUB

My grandmother stands over me
while I sit in a rusted tin tub of water.
I am dull—I felt my life was over.
Emotions had run away,
and I acted as if she was not there.
Water from the tub she drizzled over my hair.
In the bottom of the tub,
was my doubt gathered along the way.
My sorrows too—leaving me with nothing to say.
I'm almost all washed off.
All my lowliness floats on top.
The weariness that I felt
is about to be thrown out.
Me and my grandmother
tossed it on the rocks.

# IF EVER YOU NEEDED ME

If ever you needed me, I would stop time itself
just to listen to you.
If ever you needed me, I would steal away from
whatever and whomever just to be with you.
If ever you needed me, I would give up the
very thing I treasure most just to sit on the curb with you.
If ever you needed me, I would hold your troubles
and despair and wash them all away.
If ever you needed me…

RW

# TOUCHING MY EGO

You had the nerve to touch my ego
Slapping down
And attempting to slice the little I have
Esteems so high I can touch the Milky Way
You tried to take that away
Envy puffing like smoke from a bull's nose
Provoking me to lose control
Scissor deep and razor sharp
You tried to stomp on my heart
Titanium and bullet proof vest
Guarded my heart best
You might cut and I may bleed
But I cannot die you see
Touching my ego only shocked my liveliness
Giving me the strength to see the rise and fall in my chest
Nicely attempted—but I'm not an easy prey
I'm grown and strength is in my veins
Tie your hands behind your back if you ever see me again
My ego proudly stands and continues to mirror an extraordinary woman

# GOD'S LOVE

I want God's love… not the kind of love that's determined by finances.
I want God's love… not the kind of love based on lies and mischief.
I want God's love… not the kind of love that fades with time.
I want God's love… not the kind of love based on empty promises.
I want God's love… not the kind of love that leads to death.
I want God's love… the kind of love that's based on truth and character.
I want God's love… the kind of love that keeps you faithful.
I want God's love… the kind of love that keeps you humble.
I want God's love… the kind of love that keeps you safe.
I want God's love because He first loved me when I didn't love myself.

RW

# DEAR KENDRA!

I see a beautiful woman
With life's dreams and wishes
Diamonds and sapphires in her
Notebook
As she plans her life
And dreams up new beginnings
Who really knows what lies ahead
This road with many new ventures
She's afraid
But still she walks her course
Gold on her shoes
Purple on her back
Her glory down to her shoulders
Anointing
from her face
Yes—she is afraid
But still she walks
She is encouraged to go on

# MINE ENEMY

The enemy of my enemy is my friend.
I do not want to go to that place again.
It has been several months since I was there.
Several months from the looks and the stares.
Loving hearts of the world gone astray.
It may be the end of tomorrow or even today.
I have fallen victim to Babylon The Great,
but I will not let her take me or my soul to forsake.
My enemy is strong with disguises and trickery.
I was down on my knees chained in misery.
Broken free from the mockery, taunts and chains,
pulled into the light and out the rain…
The enemy of my enemy is my friend.

RW

# WALKING IN THE SUN

I need to walk in the sun
Feel the beams
Illuminating my dark-toned skin
To shine away all the darkness
That has settled within
There's a blues song
That has rocked my motion
And brightness
Has slowly been
Rolling away
I need to bath in the sun
To bath my soul
So I can sing righteous songs
And healing tones
Nations of joy
And triumphant revelations
As my story is told
Of how I was walking in the dark
Didn't know which way to go
How to turn
And discern
What's best for me
I have decided to start
With one of the most natural ways
Of healing
And that's to take a walk in the sun

# THE BOTTOM

I had to reach the bottom
to get to the top.
I thought I told you:
I will not stop.
Life sometimes
can seem out of sync.
On the way down, you
have to stop and think.
Is there a way up from
going down?
When all seems lost before
you are found.
You must crawl in the cage
before you can walk.
You may mumble in a phrase
before you can talk.
Listen and understand before you speak,
practice hard to surpass your peak.
Don't worry about how far you will fall,
just remember that you have to stand tall,
because in the midst of it all,
YOU WILL SUCCEED!

RW

# DON'T COME LOOKING FOR ME

Don't come looking for me
Cause I'll be gone
In the streets I will roam
Under a bushel
Under a tree
Please don't come looking for me
I've lost my steps
No bread crumbs to trace
Sun to the east
Sun to the north
Which way is my course
I run and I run and I run so far
"Out of the wilderness!" is what I roar
When I'm ready I'll return
With wholeness and steadiness of mind
Healed from grief and quiet sighs
Until then, I'll be gone
Into the streets
I will roam
Under a bushel
Under a tree
Please don't come looking for me

# RIGHT OF PASSAGE

I take the road for my soul alone,
A journey through hell itself as everyone must do.
Do you think you will go to heaven?
How did you live your life?
Do you even love yourself enough
to share with another soul?
I have failed my soul many a day.
My faith shaken to the very foundation
of its core. The evil one will make it tough
to get back what's rightfully mine.
I'm afraid because I turned my back
on my brother and my father.
I believed the lie and broke my lifeline
from the vine.
I pray it's not too late, because I do not
want to hear the mashing of teeth in the
darkness that awaits.
Father, I'm sorry for all of the wrongs I have made.
I'm sorry for the lies I have told.
Please forgive this sinner and let me live.
This I pray to you, father, who art in heaven...
Amen.

RW

# LOVE AT FIRST BITE

Emotions sit at the table of forever, and two people meet for the first time. He says his name, and she says hers. He can't quite stare into her big, beautiful eyes just yet because he's caught up in a thought for just a moment—a picture of a family of three. He smiles and looks at her again.

She says, "What are you looking at, cutie?"

"I'm looking at the beginning of forever."

She smiles and blows him a kiss on the winds of bliss. For the first time in the man's life, he can honestly say he feels happy.

She asks him, "Why have you come to this table at this time in your life?"

The man says, "Forever and a day I have waited for you."

She gasps and cries a silent, lonely tear. He reaches out across the table and catches it on her cheek with a napkin. "Your tear need not touch your beautiful face. I am with you forever."

"Can you fall in love with someone you just met? Can you trust someone you have no reason to trust? Can you love someone who loves you?" She asks.

The man catches his thoughts and says, "From the moment I saw you, I knew I wanted to spend the rest of my life with you."

They stare into each other's eyes and can't believe they have found each other. They order the beginning of forever and the lifetime of happiness.

Still unsure of what is transpiring, the woman says, "How can this be true? How can you be who you say you are?"

He says, "I haven't been a perfect man until I came to this place in my life and met you. Now I can be the epitome of a good man".

They toast. She says, "to love." He replies, "to love."

They gaze into each other's eyes once again. At this very moment, they are the only two people who exist in their reality. They smile at one another and hold hands. Their thoughts are one. The connection they feel surpasses the metaphysical and mental aspects of a relationship. He is her king, and she is his queen. Her smile is captured across the sands of time, and his wisdom tells him that she is his rib. She feels that this man has captured her heart and soul. She leans forward across the table of chance and caresses his forearm. He senses that this gorgeous creature from God wants a kiss to negotiate the bonding of the union. He obliges and delivers a signature kiss to her soul. The woman smiles and blushes. The man is confident—more than ever in his life. No longer afraid to take a chance because he knows within the depth of his soul that he is in love with this woman. Her eyes big, her smile warm, her nose subtle, her lips soft, and her soul genuine. They look to the heavens as they hold hands.

The man turns to the woman and says, "I promise, with God as my witness, to love you, hold you, kiss you, miss you, please you, complete you, pray with you and marry you."

She smiles and tries to wrap her arms around the man's broad shoulders. "You are the man of my dreams, my rock, my confidant, my hero, my love, my soldier, my husband and my best friend."

They finish their meal and proceed to the dance floor.

"We have been blessed," the man says.

The woman nods her head in agreement and they kiss a second time. "How did we get here?"

The man holds her tight to his chest and says, "That's not the question. The question is: where do we go from here?"

The man and the woman look at each other as they eat from each other's plates.

He stares into her beautiful blue eyes and she into his soft brown eyes.

"We were two, but now we are one."

RW

# TOMORROW'S PAST

A mixture of blurred reality caught in a dream world of confusion. A sleepless night cradled in the darkness of my bedroom. It took four hours for my alarm to go off, and I would soon be in the shower, then on my way to work. My son got upset and would not follow my instructions to pick up his dirty socks in the locker room. I was enraged at his disobedience. I smacked him on the side of his face, and this made it worse because he got up from the bench and stormed off.

The scene changed, and I was in a world that seemed to be on a stage. Nothing seemed real. Everything appeared to be made of a synthetic material, especially the trees, the rocks, and the buildings. The characters that surrounded me appeared to know one another, but I was not sure who I was or what role I was to play on that big stage. The world around me appeared to be changing somehow. Everything was crumbling around me. The world I stood on was losing its foundation and many people were fleeing to nowhere, because there was nowhere to run from the devastation that was happening. I was the only one with rational thoughts, and I accepted the fate of man that day.

But instead, I was in a new dream world that felt like an old silent film with color but no sound. I was visiting my cousin's city of good old Columbia, Missouri, when I was a mere boy of eight years old. I had always thought I hadn't met my cousin until I was in my forties, but she told me about meeting me when I was very young. Suddenly, there I was as a teenager in my cousin's city. I was walking down the street when I saw a city bus with a young boy standing in the front window of the bus. As I walked down the street with my cousins, I thought, What in the world is that kid doing? Then I realized that young kid was me. The bus came to a stop, and I wanted to talk to my younger self. But I remembered a crazy suggestion that if you ever run into yourself in a space-time continuum, you are not to interact with yourself—you could rip the whole universe apart. My younger self did something that I will never forget. He looked out the front window of the bus and he frightened me with his huge eyes that appeared to have spotted me. Then he fixated his focus to the ground. He was engaged with a small grasshopper that was alongside the bus stop in the grass. He said something that I couldn't make out. All of this dream world had been consumed in silence, until the boy shouted at the insect. "No! You can't take us all. Leave me alone, Momma!"

Then everything went black. I was back in bed with the chills and my alarm going off at 5 a.m.

RW

# THE RHYTHM

See, it was the rhythm that made him weak. It was the rhythm that broke him down to one knee. No one alive can withstand its beat because to those like you and me, the rhythm is absolutely free. See, when we first get a taste of this delightful treat, you will say and do anything, bargain and plea. See the rhythm don't give a shit about you or me; it's what you make it out to be...

Listen, I'm going to run it down by facts and not rhyme, so you can really feel me.

Addicted to love or is it like? Take a trip on the merry-go-round and see where you are when the music stops. Addicted to this rhythm like crack; he can't stop—won't stop—until the feeling is gone. See, he has to get that first thrill he felt when he chose to make that move and fell into the groove. Didn't even like her like that, but old school said, "Cut 'em deep, as many as you like. You in the game now, baby." He's hungry for the feeling; have to stop the lust; he just wants to bust one until the next time he feels the beat. See, once you start, you can't stop. Got to do the dance until the music stops. Too many hot mommas want to feel the heat, dripping wet from the tone he speaks. Just like an engine, their heat and friction create a spark and you know what happens after dark. Always after that first-time high, thinking it will be as breathtaking as that first burst. Brothas, please, let's quit lying to ourselves...Old playas as well as new playas will say anything—do anything—to feel that rhythm. We'll never get it back; all we can do is create that same situation and feel the same until we get that next victim in our range. People, WAKE UP! He wishes he had a choice before he lost control to the rhythm. Now he knows that he can't stop, but changes it to work for him. No more lying, cheating, breaking rules... See, he stopped the music and changed his tune. Live, love, prosper, be truthful to others. Most of all, be truthful to yourself... Much love to all of my friends and family. One Love.

RW

# MOMENTS IN TIME

All that we do can only be summed up as "moments in time."

You are born; you grow; you learn; you advance mentally and physically.

You make life-changing decisions that may impact your future.

Some of us will succeed in what we want to do in this lifetime.

Most of us will be too afraid to put our best foot forward.

Many of us will fall prey to our surroundings, by choice, or by getting elected to do so.

I hope you love yourself as much as you love the trouble, because we are only here for such a short moment in time.

When you play, I hope that you play hard at what you do. I don't ever want you to say I should've, would've, could've. Those three words can kill you in more ways than one.

Live in the moment; be the moment, but be responsible in that moment.

Respect yourself as well as others. Treat others how you want to be treated. Try not to hate, but participate.

You are not the first, and you surely will not be the last person to get their heart broken from a crush.

Move on to the next chapter in your life and stop waiting on that person who stopped waiting on you years ago.

Let me see that smile that I haven't seen in a while.

Focus on your creator. Let's face it, people. There is only one God who made it possible for the impossible.

Don't get left on that rowboat in the middle of the sea.

Fight that addiction to drugs, sex, lies, hate, greed, envy, lust, jealousy, and hatred.

Be the miracle God intended you to be.

You were not chosen to follow, but to lead. Lead a good life; fight the good fight, and retire, healthy, happy, and on top of your game.

We will all stop running this race at some point in our lives, so take some time while you are running to blow a few kisses and grab a drink to quench your thirst. Get your second wind and enjoy your second effort as you pass others, but always smile and encourage those beside you to keep going. You are almost there. I knew you could do it. I believed in you. I also believed in the one that gave you strength and faith to believe in yourself.

If you take one thing I've said here today with you, I hope it is this: Love yourself, respect yourself, have faith in yourself, and above all else, believe in yourself.

God helps those who helps others. Got you on that one, didn't I? We are only here for such a short while, folks, because life is a series of "moments in time."

RW

# SETTLED BY BEAUTY

Two men standing in a restaurant, face to face, having words with each other about how they feel the unction to throw and swing their hands with punches to each other's faces. Hate and anguish tear at both of them, and they are consumed with rage. Nothing and no one seem to be the bigger of their amusement.

Suddenly, the door of the restaurant opens, and the wind from the fresh crisp air blows past a woman who walks slowly into the door, cautiously, because of the loud fighting she heard as she entered. The wind brushes past the two men, and it catches their attention as they both stop to look up at the woman whose beauty captures the moment.

They stare at her as she stares back, and it seems that time has stopped. Silence fills the room. Trying not to feel embarrassed or awkward by the woman's beauty, the two men try to finish their disagreement, but now the heat of their moment is not toward each other. It is wrapped up in the beauty they both captured in this woman. The woman turns and walks away, and the two men are now stalled, now uninterested and forgetting what had them so torn.

# FOR A SPECIAL WOMAN IN MY LIFE

To a woman who has never broken my heart.
For a woman who was dearest from the start.
I can't believe, after all these years,
you still bring love and cheers.
Your smile can melt the coldest of hearts.
Your love can stop hate from tearing them apart.
Through you I have learned to open my heart to love,
to be honest, righteous, and all the above.
You have persevered through many storms,
held your family close, and kept them warm
with the love that you have shared for a long time.
I'm glad you cared about mine.
I will love you forever and ever until the very end of time,
MOM.

RW

# CHUG AND CHOKE

From dope and smoke I choke
My life is ruined
I'm always running
Looking for a small break this life can offer
When it doesn't come, I smoke and choke

From one bottle, I chug I drank
Gulping down everything -  I frustrate
Packing down and tucking away
This life I really hate
In the morning, if I'm not better, I chug and drink

Smoking and choking
Chugging and drinking
Walking around looking
Through this mess my life exists in

I need a ray that the sunshine can offer
To shun away the darkness
That invades every chance
Around every corner
I hastily wait in the dimness of light
Choking and smoking, chugging and drinking

# THE DEPTH OF ME

I spoke of a love that I once knew,
and now I know it was because of you.
My life has showed me many things,
like kisses, misses, and butterfly wings.
I cannot return to where I once was.
The wind sings with a blustering buzz.
Time backwards does not exist,
because death itself has slit his wrists.
My innocence broken, and my body too,
fighting my way back to truth and to you.
Please forgive me as I fall to my knees.
Do you love me? Can you love me more than these?
The days are long and filled with doubt,
so, I try to cope and sort it out.
The meaning of it all appears to be bleak.
I cannot fathom the depth of the peak.
Faith, Love, and Truth—
Is that deep enough for you?

RW

# ABOUT ROBERT WRIGHT

Robert wrote his first poem in the ninth grade. He chose the old form of poetry, like, "she loves me not." The poem was terrible, and he has no idea what grade he received for it. He didn't write another poem until he was a young adult and out of college. He hated writing in school because it was a constant assignment. High school was about homework and tests. College was more writing out notes and more tests.

His name is Robert Charles Everette Wright Jr. His dad liked to refer to him as the second. The reason he started writing was to express his concealed emotions. Robert lost six people to death in a six-year period. In that group of individuals were four uncles, his dad and his grandfather. He fell into a deep depression and found himself in a big black hole with no escape. He needed help, and like most people, had to swallow his pride. It was necessary, so he could find a way to move on. He decided to get help professionally.

The counselor convinced Robert to write his emotions down on paper, and then they met to discuss issues that came up in the journal. Soon, Robert began writing poetry. It was another way to express his deepest desires and his feelings. He believes he endured the pain in order to enlighten others who have been through some tough times. The reader can experience Robert's poetry and know he/she is not alone when it comes to life's aches and pains.

Through this terrible time in his life, Robert had an anchor that kept him grounded—his 4-year-old son. He was the spark of inspiration and the reason for Robert to keep on moving through life's trials and tribulations. Robert's personal struggles have made him a better person, and he shares his pain and healing in written form.

Robert says, "I write when I'm inspired to do so. I have been told that it's a blessing to be able to write, and I'm proud that I have my family and friends who believe in me."

# ABOUT
# SADERIA CARTER

I'm Saderia Carter, born in a small town called Cuthbert, Georgia, population 3,664 today. I remember spending part of my childhood in a small four-room house with my mom and dad. My brother and I would run around the house playing—me as wonder woman with aluminum foil wrapped around my wrist and my brother as superman with a towel around his neck as a cape. He loved to make that cape wave freely behind him. We had a great time in that little house, and some not so great times as well. One morning I awoke to noise from the other room—thumps and bumps and glass breaking—cries and sounds of anger.

After a while, the noises came to a halt. My mother walked in with a towel to her face while blood trickled down as she tried to control it.

"Get up Lisa and DeeDee, we got to go," I cried in fear with tears rolling down my face. My mother was hurt. We crawl into the back seat of my dad's car with dad behind the wheel. I can't remember if he said anything to her while we were driving, however, she sniffled back tears.

We arrive at the emergency room drop off area; Mom walked in and disappeared behind the emergency room doors. My brother and I sat quietly in the back seat with worry and confusion.

Later, we arrived at my grandmother's house, who took care of us while my mother attended to her wounds.

That was many years ago. I was around five and my younger brother around the age of 3. I grew up and used my past as my strength and force to be the woman I feel I am today. I've since relocated to Nebraska. I have experienced my own trials and tribulations, as we all have in our own way. We are all walking our own path.

After going through my own divorce with two children, the heaviness of my heart was great. I decided that I could drown in despair or figure out a way to help myself; so I picked up a pen and paper and started to write. As the words began to flow, I began to feel a little better.

Two of my closest friends were also using poetry as a way of connecting, healing, and expressing themselves, so we were always sharing with each other. They were my best support system and remain so to this day.

I hope you enjoy all the passion that has pressed through my heart and mind as you read *Amalgamation*. Thank you for walking with me through this journey.

www.ingramcontent.com/pod-product-compliance
Lightning Source LLC
LaVergne TN
LVHW082059090426
835512LV00038B/2575